MOTOR-CYCLES

Alain Chirinian

JULIAN 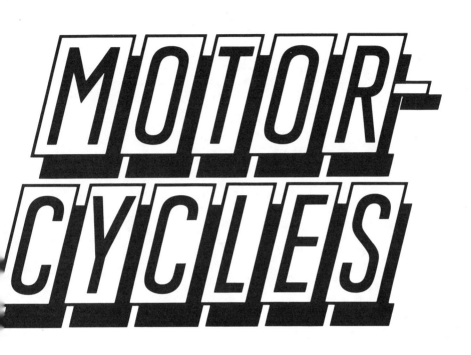 MESSNER

An Important Notice for the Reader

You are not allowed by law to operate a car or a motorcycle without a driver's license. The laws of your state or country will tell you how old you must be and what tests you must pass in order to get a license to drive. In the meantime, you can enjoy reading about cars or motorcycles in this book. Please wear a safety helmet when operating a motorcycle.

The information in this book is based on the author's research and information received from the manufacturers of some of the cars and motorcycles. The specifications for the cars and motorcycles are general and may not apply to every car or motorcycle and every model that appears in the book.

Published by Julian Messner, a division of
Silver Burdett Press, Inc., Simon & Schuster, Inc.,
Prentice Hall Bldg., Englewood Cliffs, NJ 07632.

JULIAN MESSNER and colophon are trademarks of
Simon & Schuster, Inc.
Manufactured in the United States of America.

(Lib. ed.) 10 9 8 7 6 5 4 3 2 1
(Paper ed.) 10 9 8 7 6 5 4 3 2 1

Library of Congress Cataloging-in-Publication Data

Chirinian, Alain.
  Motorcycles / Alain Chirinian.
    p. cm. — (Tough wheels)
  Summary: Describes fourteen top motorcycles of today, including the Suzuki GSX-R1100, the BMW R100RT, and the Yamaha FZR-750R.
    ISBN 0-671-68029-3 (lib. bdg.); ISBN 0-671-68034-X (pbk.)
    1. Motorcycles—Juvenile literature. [1. Motorcycles.]
  I. Title. II. Series: Chirinian, Alain. Tough wheels.
TL440.C463 1989
629.2'275—dc19   88-38358
                                                                    CIP
                                                                     AC

Photo credits and acknowledgments

Pages 6 and 10 courtesy of American Suzuki Motor Corporation
Pages 14 and 61 courtesy of Kawasaki Motors Corp., U.S.A.
Pages 18, 21, 22, and 26 courtesy of BMW of North America, Inc.
Pages 30, 33, 34, and 37 courtesy of Harley-Davidson, Inc.
Pages 38, 41, 42, 46, and 49 courtesy of Yamaha Motor Corporation, U.S.A.
Pages 13, 29, 54, and 58 from Motorcyclist Magazine/Petersen Publishing Company
Pages 9, 17, 25, 45, 50, 53, and 57 by Rich Cox/Slide Action

TABLE OF CONTENTS

SUZUKI GSXR-1100

 PERFORMANCE:
Zero to 60 MPH: Approximately 3.2 seconds
1/4 Mile Acceleration: 10.90 seconds at 125.0 MPH
Maximum Speed: 155 MPH

SPECIFICATIONS

 ENGINE:

Type: Oil-cooled four cylinder
Valve Gear: Dual overhead camshafts, four valves
per cylinder
Displacement: 1032 cc
Compression Ratio: 10.0:1
Horsepower: 100+ at 9500 RPM

CHASSIS:

Frame: Square tube, aluminum alloy
Wheels: 2.75 x 18-inch front, 4.50 x 18-inch rear
Tires: 110/80V18 front, 160/70V18 rear
Seat Height: 31 inches
Front Suspension: Telescopic fork, 41-mm diameter
Rear Suspension: Single shock, aluminum swingarm
Front Brakes: Dual disc
Rear Brakes: Single disc

Born on the Racetrack

You can tell just by looking at it that the Suzuki GSXR-1100 is a streetbike that was born on the racetrack. Suzuki developed this machine with two things in mind: the lightest possible weight, and the highest level of horsepower in one package. This combination made the GSXR-1100 one of the fastest motorcycles ever made.

Oil-Cooled Engine

Every part of the GSXR-1100 shows how Suzuki did its best not to add any extra weight when designing the bike. They decided not to use a regular water cooling system on the engine, because that would have been too heavy. Instead, the engineers developed an oil cooling system that was much lighter and worked just as well to keep the engine from overheating.

New Alloy

The chassis of the GSXR-1100 may be the most important reason for the incredible performance of this machine. Suzuki and another Japanese company designed a new aluminum alloy for the frame of the GSXR. This metal is so light and strong that the frame only weighs a few pounds, but still allows a powerful engine to be used without breaking under the strain.

On the Road

The only time the ride of the GSXR-1100 is really comfortable is at speeds well over the legal limit. The low, "clip-on" style handlebars force the rider to stretch over the large gas tank. The footpegs are raised high off the ground for clearance when leaning over. Suzuki builds other great motorcycles if you want comfort. But if you want one of the fastest ways to get around a racetrack, the Suzuki GSXR-1100 is your ticket.

SUZUKI GSX-1100 KATANA

 PERFORMANCE:
Zero to 60 MPH: Approximately 3.2 seconds
1/4 Mile Acceleration: Approximately 10.95 seconds
at 124.5 MPH
Maximum Speed: 153 MPH

SPECIFICATIONS

 ENGINE:

Type: Oil-cooled four cylinder
Valve Gear: Dual overhead camshafts, four valves
per cylinder
Displacement: 1127 cc
Compression Ratio: 10.1:1
Horsepower: 100+ at 9000 RPM

CHASSIS:

Frame: Square tube steel
Wheels: 2.75 × 16-inch front, 3.50 × 16-inch rear
Tires: 120/80V16 front, 150/80V16 rear
Seat Height: 29.9 inches
Front Suspension: Telescopic fork, 41-mm diameter
Rear Suspension: Single shock, adjustable
Front Brakes: Dual disc
Rear Brakes: Single disc

The Best of Both Worlds

Imagine Suzuki's powerful GSXR-1100: incredibly fast, but uncomfortable at most speeds. Now imagine the performance of the GSXR combined with features that help you ride the motorcycle for miles in comfort. That is the new GSX-1100 Katana. With an engine of the same design as the sports model GSXR-1100, and many convenience features from Suzuki's touring motorcycles, the Katana has the best of both racing and touring in one machine.

Civilized Sportbike

''Katana'' means fighting sword in Japanese, and the high performance of this GSX model makes it a fighting machine. But the Katana offers comfort as well as the performance of the standard sports model GSXR. The rear suspension is adjustable for a soft or hard ride. The handlebars are higher up so the rider doesn't have to bend over to reach them. Even the windshield adjusts up and down by a small switch on the handlebar!

Larger Engine

The engine in the Katana was made even larger to give it a performance close to that of the lighter GSXR model. The fairing keeps the wind off the rider's body and helps the bike cut through the wind to a top speed of over 150 miles per hour!

All-Steel Chassis

Instead of the aluminum alloy of the GSXR-1100 frame, the Katana uses a steel chassis that wraps around the engine like a racebike's. Since the Katana isn't meant to be used on a racetrack, the few extra pounds from a steel frame make very little difference in its performance.

On the Road

After your first ride on the Katana, you'll see that it offers the same arm-pulling acceleration of its racer-replica brother, the GSXR-1100. In less time than it takes to read this sentence, you can rocket up to almost 100 miles per hour! At the same time, the big Suzuki is quiet, comfortable, and fun to ride.

KAWASAKI ZX-10 NINJA

 PERFORMANCE:
Zero to 60 MPH: Approximately 2.9 seconds
1/4 Mile Acceleration: Approximately 10.70 seconds
at 130 MPH
Maximum Speed: 170 MPH

SPECIFICATIONS

 ENGINE:

Type: Liquid-cooled four cylinder
Valve Gear: Dual overhead camshafts, four valves
per cylinder
Displacement: 997 cc
Compression Ratio: 11.0:1
Horsepower: 120 at 11,000 RPM

CHASSIS:

Frame: Square tube aluminum
Wheels: 3.50 × 17-inch front, 4.50 × 18-inch rear
Tires: 120/70VR17 front, 160/VR6018 rear
Seat Height: 31 inches
Front Suspension: Telescopic fork, 41-mm diameter
Rear Suspension: Single shock, aluminum swingarm
Front Brakes: Dual disc
Rear Brakes: Single disc

The Fastest Motorcycle

For years Kawasaki has had the reputation of building the toughest and fastest motorcycles around. So when Kawasaki's engineers began to work on the newest Ninja, they knew from the beginning that it had to be the fastest motorcycle money could buy. They succeeded. Just how fast is the ZX-10? How does 170 miles per hour sound?

Wind-Cheating Shape

The ZX-10 may be the best-looking Kawasaki ever. Its wind-cheating lines form a quiet envelope of air around the rider, even at top speed. The fairing helps the motorcycle and rider slice through the air with confidence. The turn signals are part of the body and don't stick out to slow things down. This Kawasaki seems as if it was carved out of a single piece, instead of many smaller pieces put together.

A Better Engine

To build the fastest motorcycle, the engineers at Kawasaki had to squeeze every last ounce of horsepower they could from the Ninja 1000 engine. They did this by making many of the parts lighter and thinner so the engine could spin faster. At the same time, they fine-tuned the cylinder head for a better flame in the combustion chamber.

New Chassis

The chassis of the ZX-10 is all new. It is made of all aluminum, with very thick "box-section" tubing for strength. Triple disc brakes slow it down from light speed without complaint. The Kawasaki also has larger wheels and radial tires so that the machine remains stable.

Comfort on the Road

When you put a leg over the seat, you notice that you don't have to crouch too low to reach the handlebars, as you do on some bikes. You feel good, knowing that there isn't a motorcycle around that can go faster—except maybe another ZX-10 Ninja!

17

BMW R100RT

 **PERFORMANCE:**
Zero to 60 MPH: 5.0 seconds
1/4 Mile Acceleration: 13.5 seconds at 97.5 MPH
Maximum Speed: 120 MPH

SPECIFICATIONS

 ENGINE:

Type: Horizontally opposed two cylinder
Valve Gear: Pushrod operated, two valves per
cylinder
Displacement: 980 cc
Compression Ratio: 8.5:1
Horsepower: 60 at 6500 RPM

CHASSIS:

Frame: Round tube steel
Wheels: 2.50 × 18-inch front, 2.50 × 18-inch rear
Tires: 90/90V18 front, 120/90V18 rear
Seat Height: 31.5 inches
Front Suspension: Telescopic fork, 38.5-mm diameter
Rear Suspension: Monolever, single-sided swingarm
Front Brakes: Dual disc
Rear Brakes: Single disc

Highest Quality

For years, BMW has been a maker of two-cylinder (or ''twin'' cylinder), shaft-drive motorcycles. Over this time, the company has developed and refined the same basic engine until they have gotten it just about perfect. The R100RT is built by highly skilled craftsmen in Germany, and the BMW name guarantees it is a machine of the highest quality.

A Modern Machine

In some ways, the R100RT reminds you of the motor-cycles from the past, when machines were simple to work on and were built by hand. But the R100 is a very modern motorcycle in many ways—from its newly designed rear suspension system to its wind-tunnel designed fairing.

''Boxer'' Engine

This BMW's engine is known as the ''Boxer'' because of the location of its two cylinders. The cylinders face opposite directions, like two boxers in opposite corners in a ring. Over the years, this basic engine has been improved to make it smoother, faster, and quieter than most other ''twins.'' It is simple to main-tain and lasts for a very long time.

Shaft Drive

The rear wheel of the R100RT, as on all BMWs, is driven by a shaft. Cars are also shaft-driven. Like bicycles, most motorcycles use a chain, which must be tightened and lubricated—something that the BMW rider doesn't have to do. On a long-distance machine like the R100RT, it's nice not to worry about lubricating a chain every few thousand miles.

Riding the R100RT

You feel warm inside the fairing of the big BMW. The motor purrs from beneath you like a friendly cat. This machine can be ridden almost anywhere, for as long as you like. The BMW R100RT—there is nothing else quite like it on the road today.

BMW K100RS

 PERFORMANCE:
Zero to 60 MPH: 4.5 seconds
1/4 Mile Acceleration: 12.6 seconds at 105.5 MPH
Maximum Speed: 135 MPH

SPECIFICATIONS

 ENGINE:

Type: Water-cooled four cylinder
Valve Gear: Dual overhead camshafts, two valves
per cylinder
Displacement: 987 cc
Compression Ratio: 10.0:1
Horsepower: 85 at 8000 RPM

CHASSIS:

Frame: Round tube steel
Wheels: 2.50 × 18-inch front, 2.75 × 17-inch rear
Tires: 100/90V18 front, 130/90V17 rear
Seat Height: 32.8 inches
Front Suspension: Telescopic fork, 41-mm diameter
Rear Suspension: Monolever, single shock with one-
sided swingarm
Front Brakes: Dual disc
Rear Brakes: Single disc

The First Four

The K100 was the first four-cylinder motorcycle from the company famous for its "boxer" twins. This BMW was even named motorcycle of the year in Japan when it was first introduced! The K100RS is the sporty model of the K100 series machines. Its fuel-injected motor is designed for 135 mile-per-hour performance on the roads of Germany, and shaft drive keeps it all under control.

Monolever Suspension

The rear suspension of the K100RS has just one shock absorber and spring. While many motorcycles have "single shock" rear suspensions, their shocks and springs are in the center of the motorcycle's swingarm. The BMW "monolever," on the other hand, is mounted on the side, a very unusual design that helps control the shaft drive.

Sideways Engine

Instead of being upright as on other four-cylinder bikes, the K100RS engine is mounted sideways! This makes it easier to work on the engine while it is still in the frame. The engine is one of the few that have electronic fuel injection for smoother, more efficient running.

Out of the Wind

At the speeds the K100RS is capable of going, the force of the wind is very strong. The fairing of this BMW is designed to keep the rider protected from the cold wind. The windshield is tall enough to push the rushing air over the rider's head and keep things quiet. Mirrors are mounted in front of the rider's hands to help keep them warm.

On the Road

This sporty BMW has a lower riding position and a stiffer suspension for control when cornering. But the ride is still BMW-smooth over the roughest pavement. The shaft drive needs no adjustment, and the smooth engine cruises at high speeds easily, without strain.

BMW K75S

 PERFORMANCE:
Zero to 60 MPH: 4.1 seconds
1/4 Mile Acceleration: 12.80 seconds at 103.1 MPH
Maximum Speed: 120 MPH

SPECIFICATIONS

 ENGINE:
Type: Water-cooled three cylinder
Valve Gear: Dual overhead camshafts, two valves
per cylinder
Displacement: 740 cc
Compression Ratio: 10.5:1
Horsepower: 75 at 8500 RPM

CHASSIS:
Frame: Round tube steel
Wheels: 2.50 × 18-inch front, 2.75 × 17-inch rear
Tires: 100/90V18 front, 130/90V17 rear
Seat Height: 32.8 inches
Front Suspension: Telescopic fork, 41-mm diameter
Rear Suspension: Single shock, monolever, single-
sided swingarm
Front Brakes: Dual disc
Rear Brakes: Single disc

Missing One Cylinder

The 740-cc K75S owes most of its success to its big brother, the K100. In fact, this bike has basically the same engine as the K100, only it's missing one cylinder! The rest of this three-cylinder machine shares many parts with the K100, however, and that's good. The same strong triple disc brakes and tubular frame hold things together at Autobahn speeds. This BMW model may be the most sporting ever!

Lighter Weight

The lighter weight of the three-cylinder K75S means it is easier to handle in tight corners than the larger K100. The smaller, sculpted fairing weighs less than the K100 fairing and offers almost as much protection from the wind. The smaller, lighter engine has fewer parts than four-cylinder motorcycles, and this keeps the weight of the K75S down as well.

Work of Art

The K75S looks unlike any BMW before it. The high-quality paint shines on the aluminum gas tank. The narrow fairing is built from the highest-quality materials. There are no bulky wires around the instruments. And the lower cowling helps make this motorcycle look like it's moving even when parked!

Three-Cylinder Engine

The K75S is the only three-cylinder motorcycle sold in the United States. Three-cylinder motorcycles are very rare. Usually they are based on a four-cylinder design, minus one cylinder. One less cylinder allows the rider to have most of the performance of a four-cylinder machine, with fewer moving parts in the engine and lighter weight.

HARLEY-DAVIDSON XLH883 SPORTSTER

 PERFORMANCE:
Zero to 60 MPH: 5.0 seconds
1/4 Mile Acceleration: 14 seconds at 93 MPH
Maximum Speed: 110 MPH

SPECIFICATIONS

 ENGINE:

Type: Air-cooled V-twin
Valve Gear: Two valves per cylinder, pushrod actuated
Displacement: 883 cc
Compression Ratio: 9.0:1
Horsepower: 50 at 6000 RPM

CHASSIS:

Frame: Round tube steel
Wheels: 19-inch front, 16-inch rear, cast aluminum
Tires: MJ90-19 front, MT90-16 rear
Seat Height: 29.5 inches
Front Suspension: Telescopic fork, 39-mm diameter
Rear Suspension: Dual shock, steel swingarm
Front Brakes: Single disc
Rear Brakes: Single disc

Pure Harley-Davidson

When many people think of a motorcycle, they think of a Harley-Davidson. Harleys have always been large, V-twin-engined motorcycles. The 883 is pure Harley-Davidson, and one of the best that the Milwaukee company has ever built.

"Evolution" Engine

The engine in the 883 is one of Harley-Davidson's newest designs. Its alloy construction is beautiful to look at, while inside, it makes more power and is quieter than ever before. The engineers at Harley-Davidson used computers to help them design the "evolution" engine in the 883 Sportster for strength and durability.

No Extra Gadgets

Unlike many motorcycles today, the 883 Sportster doesn't have anything like a digital clock, or a fuel gauge, or even a tachometer! This motorcycle has only the things that the rider really needs, like a speedometer and turn signals. Even the seat is built for just one person—the rider!

Showroom Success

The 883 Sportster, like most Harleys, is a very popular bike to own. The beauty of this machine is in how "real" everything looks: The fenders are real metal, not plastic. The engine isn't hidden by a brightly colored fairing. This motorcycle sounds like only a Harley-Davidson can.

On the Road

Push the starter and the 883 slowly rumbles to life. Open the throttle and the V-twin engine pushes you back in your seat. You don't seem to notice the missing tachometer, clock, or other gadgets. That is what makes the 883 such a special motorcycle. It is all that many people could ever want.

33

HARLEY-DAVIDSON HERITAGE SOFTAIL

 PERFORMANCE:
Zero to 60 MPH: 5.0 seconds
1/4 Mile Acceleration: 14.05 seconds at 93 MPH
Maximum Speed: 115 MPH

SPECIFICATIONS

 ENGINE:

Type: Air-cooled two cylinder
Valve Gear: Two valves per cylinder, pushrod
actuated
Displacement: 1338 cc
Compression Ratio: 8.5:1
Horsepower: 74 at 5400 RPM

CHASSIS:

Frame: Round tube steel
Wheels: 3.00 × 16-inch front, 3.00 × 16-inch rear
Tires: MT90S-16 front, MT90S-16 rear
Seat Height: 26.5 inches
Front Suspension: Telescopic fork, 41-mm diameter
Rear Suspension: Dual shock absorbers
Front Brakes: Single disc
Rear Brakes: Single disc

Classic Styling

This Harley-Davidson may be the coolest machine on the road today. Nothing looks quite like it, except for older, "antique" motorcycles. Harley found that this classic look was so popular, it brought back an older model, updating it for today's riders. It may seem like a 1950 model from far away, but the Heritage Softail has many modern features.

Belt Drive

Instead of the chain drive or shaft drive of other motorcycles, the Heritage Softail uses a toothed rubber belt to drive the rear wheel. The rubber belt needs few adjustments, like a shaft drive system, and is simple to build, like a chain drive system. Belt drive has the best qualities of both systems.

Huge Engine

The Softail has a 1338-cc engine; that's bigger than some car engines! This "evolution" engine has two cylinders, and is in the shape of a "vee," like all Harley-Davidson engines. The rest of the motorcycle is big, too. It's not easy to make turns at low speed. The Softail is meant for experienced riders only.

Spoked Wheels

Most motorcycles today have aluminum, "mag" style wheels, but this Harley has spoked wheels, like a bicycle. In the 1950s, all motorcycles had spoked wheels. Today the Heritage Softail is one of the few street motorcycles that use this style of wheel.

On the Seat

Sit on the Heritage Softail and you notice how low to the ground this bike is, like all "cruisers." It may look like there aren't any rear shock absorbers, but they are hidden under the bike! When you ride this bike, people will ask you what year it was made. They won't believe that it's brand-new!

YAMAHA V-MAX

 **PERFORMANCE:**
Zero to 60 MPH: 2.85 seconds
1/4 Mile Acceleration: 10.80 seconds at 128 MPH
Maximum Speed: 140 MPH

SPECIFICATIONS

 ENGINE:
Type: Water-cooled V-four
Valve Gear: Dual overhead camshafts, four valves
per cylinder
Displacement: 1198 cc
Compression Ratio: 10.5:1
Horsepower: 130 at 9000 RPM

CHASSIS:
Frame: Tubular steel
Wheels: 2.15 × 18-inch front, 3.50 × 15-inch rear
Tires: 110/90V18 front, 150/90V15 rear
Seat Height: 30.1 inches
Front Suspension: Telescopic fork, 40-mm diameter
Rear Suspension: Dual shocks, with coil over springs
Front Brakes: Dual disc
Rear Brakes: Single disc

Hot-Rod Motorcycle

The V-Max is a rocket on wheels. It is so fast that it hurts to think about it. When you crack the throttle, you can spin the rear tire just like a dragster. The V-Max is a hot-rod motorcycle that you can buy from your local Yamaha dealer!

Fake Gas Tank

The gas tank on the V-Max is not where you think it is. What looks like the gas tank is really a plastic cover for the airbox. The real gas tank is located under the seat. The gas under the seat helps keep the weight of the V-Max low on the back end for better traction when accelerating fast.

Strong Chassis

The chassis of the V-Max had to be very strong to handle the incredible power of this street monster. The suspension is soft enough for a comfortable ride on the street, but stiff enough not to bounce around. Massive disc brakes are there to slow the V-Max down from hyper-speed. The rear tire is wider than many car tires!

Beefed-Up Engine

The 1198-cc engine of the V-Max is a beefed-up version of Yamaha's big touring engine, from the Venture model. Special metals were used to strengthen the engine to stand up to the extra heat and stress from this high-horsepower engine. The V-Max also uses a "V-Boost" intake system for extra power at high RPM.

YAMAHA FZR-750R

 PERFORMANCE:
Zero to 60 MPH: 4.0 seconds
1/4 Mile Acceleration: 11.50 seconds at 119.0 MPH
Maximum Speed: 150 MPH

SPECIFICATIONS

 ENGINE:
Type: Water-cooled four cylinder
Valve Gear: Dual overhead camshafts, five valves
per cylinder
Displacement: 749 cc
Compression Ratio: 11.2:1
Horsepower: 95 at 11,500 RPM

CHASSIS:
Frame: "Deltabox" aluminum alloy
Wheels: 3.50 × 17-inch front, 4.50 × 17-inch rear
Tires: 120/70VR17 front, 160/60VR18 rear
Front Suspension: Telescopic fork, 41-mm diameter
Rear Suspension: Aluminum swingarm with single
shock
Front Brakes: Dual disc
Rear Brakes: Single disc

Landmark

Yamaha's FZ-750 was a landmark motorcycle when it was introduced in 1985. In one brilliant stroke of engineering, it shattered the hopes of the competition. With an engine design using the most advanced technology, Yamaha achieved the highest possible performance for a streetbike of its size.

Five-Valve Engine

While most high-performance motorcycles use a four-valve-per-cylinder head design, the engine in the FZ-750 was the first in the world with *five* valves per cylinder. This means more air and fuel in the combustion chamber, and that spells HORSEPOWER.

Square-Tube Frame

To go with all of this power, Yamaha had to build a chassis to help guide a rider around corners safely. To do this, the engineers at Yamaha designed a special steel frame made of square tubes that can take almost any strain. Special brakes, wheels, and tires make the FZ-750 quick in turns and stable at maximum speed.

On the Road

Today you can buy the new, limited-edition
FZR-750R. Riding the FZR is an even more thrilling
experience than the FZ-750. As you swing your leg
over the seat, you notice how low the crouch is to
the handlebars. The large tachometer reads to
14,000 RPM. The speedometer goes to 160 miles per
hour. You feel like a roadracer before even starting
the engine!

YAMAHA FZR-1000

 **PERFORMANCE:**
Zero to 60 MPH: 2.7 seconds
1/4 Mile Acceleration: 10.69 seconds at 128 MPH
Maximum Speed: 160 MPH

SPECIFICATIONS

 ENGINE:

Type: Water-cooled four cylinder
Valve Gear: Dual overhead camshafts, five valves
per cylinder
Displacement: 998 cc
Compression Ratio: 11.2:1
Horsepower: 125 at 11,500 RPM

CHASSIS:

Frame: ''Deltabox'' aluminum alloy
Wheels: 3.50 × 17-inch front, 4.50 × 18-inch rear
Tires: 120/70VR17 front, 160/60VR18 rear
Seat Height: 30.1 inches
Front Suspension: Telescopic fork, 41-mm diameter
Rear Suspension: Single shock with aluminum
swingarm
Front Brakes: Dual disc
Rear Brakes: Single disc

High Technology

The Yamaha FZR-1000 is packed with high technology. The engineers at Yamaha have used computers to create a motorcycle of the highest possible performance. This motorcycle is a super performer on the street and the racetrack. Each part of this machine was designed with high speed in mind.

Racebike for the Street

The FZR-1000 is really just a racebike with lights, turn signals, and street tires. It has a very firm suspension for cornering control at high speeds. Its five-valve-per-cylinder design has been proven excellent by the FZR-1000's smaller brother, the FZ-750. The seating position is comfortable only at high speeds, when the rushing wind helps to hold up the rider.

"Deltabox" Frame

One look at the frame and you can see that Yamaha engineers take cornering and stability very seriously. The frame design is known as the "Deltabox" and is one of the most advanced chassis on a street motorcycle. The suspension and brakes are also race-quality pieces that are hard to find on a street machine.

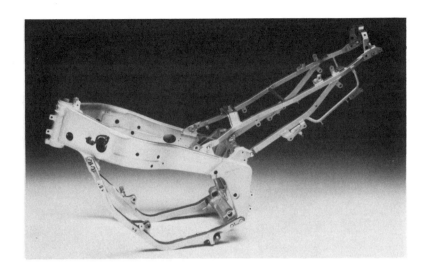

"Genesis" Engine

The FZR's five-valve-per-cylinder engine is called the "Genesis" by Yamaha. It is of a similar design to the FZ-750 engine the company has built for several years. This design helps the Yamaha put out lots of horsepower and stay together after a very long race. The engine is so tough that it only needs a tune-up every 17,000 miles!

HONDA CBR1000 HURRICANE

 PERFORMANCE:
Zero to 60 MPH: 2.9 seconds
1/4 Mile Acceleration: 10.95 seconds at 126 MPH
Maximum Speed: 160 MPH

SPECIFICATIONS

 ENGINE:

Type: Water-cooled four cylinder
Valve Gear: Dual overhead camshafts, four valves
per cylinder
Displacement: 998 cc
Compression Ratio: 10.5:1
Horsepower: 120 at 10,500 RPM

CHASSIS:

Frame: Square tube steel
Wheels: 2.50 × 17-inch front, 3.50 × 18-inch rear
Tires: 110/80V17 front, 140/V17 rear
Seat Height: 31.5 inches
Front Suspension: Telescopic fork, 41-mm diameter
Rear Suspension: Single shock, steel swingarm
Front Brakes: Dual disc
Rear Brakes: Single disc

Super Sport Machine

The Honda Hurricane is a very well-known motorcyle by now. It became famous when it was first introduced and went over 160 miles per hour! But the most unusual thing about the 1000 Hurricane is that it can go, stop, and handle like a racebike and still be a very comfortable machine to ride on the street.

Enclosed Engine

The first thing people notice about Honda's biggest Hurricane is that the engine is covered up by the plastic fairing. One of the main reasons the engine is not out in the open is to help the bike cut through the wind. An engine out in the wind creates "drag," which can slow down the motorcycle. Honda wanted to build one of the fastest machines around, so they covered the engine with the fairing.

"Standard" Design

The Hurricane uses a standard four-cylinder engine design, meaning that it does not use the most advanced technology. This doesn't mean the Honda isn't just as good as those high-tech bikes—it's better than most! The engineers at Honda somehow built a motorcycle that uses older technology with very high performance, but at a lower cost for the buyer. Now that's high performance!

Easy to Ride

The Hurricane is crammed full of performance items. Every inch of space on this motorcycle is used to keep the machine compact and easy to handle. There is plenty of room for the rider, however. The 1000 Hurricane is an easy machine to ride.

On the Road

The Hurricane has one of the smoothest four-cylinder motors in motorcycling. It has light steering for a machine of its size, and you feel confident when cornering. The suspension does a great job on the bumps and potholes in the road. If you wanted to, you could take it to the racetrack right now—you might even win!

HONDA GL1500/6 GOLDWING

 PERFORMANCE:
Zero to 60 MPH: 5.0 seconds
1/4 Mile Acceleration: 13.3 seconds at 98.0 MPH
Maximum Speed: 110 MPH

SPECIFICATIONS

 ENGINE:
Type: Water-cooled six cylinder
Valve Gear: Single overhead camshaft, two valves per cylinder
Displacement: 1520 cc
Compression Ratio: 9.8:1
Horsepower: 95 at 5000 RPM

CHASSIS:
Frame: Tubular steel
Wheels: 3.00 × 18-inch front, 3.50 × 16-inch rear
Tires: 130/70H-18 front, 160/70H-16 rear
Seat Height: 30.6 inches
Front Suspension: Telescopic fork, 41-mm diameter
Rear Suspension: Dual shocks, air pressure adjustable
Front Brakes: Dual disc
Rear Brakes: Single disc

Comfort Like a Car

The new Honda Goldwing is one of the big "touring" bikes that are built especially for traveling great distances. The Goldwing is the original of these luxury touring machines, and the latest version is also the best of its type. The new six-cylinder engine and comfort-related gadgets make the new Goldwing one of the best machines to travel on—it's as comfortable as a car!

Six-Cylinder Engine

The new Goldwing engine is probably the smoothest in motorcycling. You can balance a coin on it, it's so smooth! The new engine makes plenty of power, too. The Goldwing needs a powerful engine—it carries two people and a lot of supplies that can get very heavy. This engine is unlike any other in motorcycling.

Reverse Gear

The Goldwing is so heavy that it has a reverse gear for backing up out of tight places. The electric starter motor, not the regular engine, is used to push the Goldwing backward. There is also a four-speaker stereo on the big Honda, so you can crank up your favorite tunes when you are riding!

Built for Two

Many people who ride Goldwings like to carry a passenger with them. Honda designed a special seat in the rear of the bike just for the passenger. The seat is adjustable, and the passenger can look over the rider's head and see the road. There is room in the trunk for all the gear you would want to pack.

On the Road

The Goldwing is not hard to ride once you get going. There is a pocket of still, quiet air around you as you pick up speed, and you can feel hardly any vibration from the engine. The Honda Goldwing is one of the most comfortable ways to travel on a motorcycle.

KAWASAKI KLR-650

 PERFORMANCE:
Zero to 60 MPH: 4.7 seconds
1/4 Mile Acceleration: 13.8 seconds at 89 MPH
Maximum Speed: 110 MPH

SPECIFICATIONS

 ENGINE:

Type: Water-cooled single cylinder
Valve Gear: Dual overhead camshafts, four valves
per cylinder
Displacement: 651 cc
Compression Ratio: 9.5:1
Horsepower: 40 at 7000 RPM

CHASSIS:

Frame: Tubular steel
Wheels: 1.60 × 21-inch front, 2.50 × 17-inch rear
Tires: 90/90-21 front, 130/80-17 rear
Seat Height: 35 inches
Front Suspension: Telescopic fork, 38-mm diameter
Rear Suspension: Single shock, steel aluminum
swingarm
Front Brakes: Single disc
Rear Brakes: Single disc

Two Motorcycles in One

Imagine riding your favorite streetbike on a canyon road. Suddenly, you see a sign telling you that the road is about to end. There is only a dirt path leading up the mountain. On most motorcycles you would have to stop and turn around. But on the Kawasaki KLR-650, you have nothing to worry about—it's a streetbike and a dirtbike in one machine!

The Biggest Single

The KLR-650 has the largest single-cylinder engine you can buy in the USA. It has one huge piston that pumps out lots of horsepower and stump-pulling torque for riding under any conditions. Water cooling keeps the engine temperature under control, and an electric starter promises easier starting than having to kickstart the big single.

Ultimate Handling

The tires may not be as wide as a sportbike's, but they don't need to be because this Kawasaki is very light. It can easily be flicked back and forth through corners, with the suspension soaking up any bumps in the road. Its strong engine helps you slingshot out of any corner like the best of the sportbikes.

Unlimited Cornering Clearance

The KLR is so high off the ground that none of its parts can touch the ground no matter how far you lean when cornering. The bike is narrow because it has only one cylinder, and you can get through turns much more safely than on some of the heavier motorcyles.

Dirtbiking the KLR-650

If you want to get off the highway and ride in the dirt, the KLR is ready to take you there. Its special tires were designed to grip the dirt as well as the pavement. You can fly off jumps just like the motocross racers. You can pop wheelies all day long on this bike!

GLOSSARY

Air Box—A box holding an air cleaner that filters the air before it gets to the engine.

Aluminum Alloy—A mixture of aluminum and other metals that is usually stronger than plain aluminum.

Belt Drive—A belt connected to the engine that brings power to the rear wheel of the motorcycle. Harley-Davidson uses belt drive on some models.

Chain Drive—A chain connected to the engine that brings power to the rear wheel. Chain drive is used on most motorcycles.

Chassis—A system of components that links the engine and rider to the road. The chassis is made up of the frame, wheels, brakes, and suspension.

Combustion Chamber—A chamber above each piston where an explosion occurs, caused by fuel being ignited by the spark plug. This explosion forces the pistons to move, and this process turns the engine.

Compression Ratio—The ratio of how tight the piston compresses the air in the combustion chamber to the volume of the cylinder.

Cylinder—A round hole inside the engine where a piston moves up and down.

Cylinder Head—A block of metal covering the top of the engine above the cylinders. It contains the combustion chamber, valves, valve springs, camshaft, and other parts.

Disc Brake—A flat, round disc attached to the wheel that is "grabbed" by a caliper when the brake lever is pulled.

Displacement—The size of the engine, which depends on the size of the pistons.

Drag—The amount that the motorcycle resists the air when pushing through it. A motorcycle with low drag cuts through the air better than one with more drag.

Five Valves per Cylinder—A cylinder head design that uses five valves to control intake and exhaust in the combustion chamber. This design is used by Yamaha for its "Genesis" engines.

Frame—A cage made of metal that holds the engine and suspension together rigidly.

Fuel Injection—A fuel injection system electronically controls the mixture of fuel and air entering the combustion chamber. Fuel injection is used on some motorcycles, such as BMWs.

Horsepower—A measurement of how much power an engine can put out.

Monolever Suspension—The single-shock rear suspension design used in BMW models.

Oil Cooling System—A method of cooling the engine of certain high-performance Suzuki motorcycles. Instead of water, as in most other motorcycles, oil is used to circulate around the engine and keep it cool.

Piston—A roundish piece of metal that moves up and down inside the cylinder. The piston is forced to move by an explosion in the combustion chamber. Usually, the bigger the piston, the more powerful the engine. Piston size is used to calculate the size of the engine.

Radial Tire—A type of tire that uses specially shaped materials inside for durability as well as excellent grip when cornering.

Shaft Drive—A round metal shaft that brings power from the engine to the rear wheel by a connection to the engine on one side and the rear wheel on the other side. All BMWs use a shaft drive system.

Shock Absorber—A metal tube that slides inside another metal tube. The shock absorber contains heavy oil and sometimes air or other gases. It absorbs bumps in the road so the rider is more comfortable and has better control of the motorcycle.

Starter Motor—A small electric motor connected to the engine. It starts the engine instead of the rider having to kickstart the motorcycle.

Suspension System—A system of levers and shock absorbers that mount the wheels of the motorcycle to the frame. The suspension absorbs bumps in the road, allowing the rider to have a smooth ride.

Throttle Valve—A valve in the carburetor that controls the amount of fuel entering the engine from the fuel tank. On a motorcycle, the "throttle" is controlled by the right-hand twist grip. You open the throttle to increase speed by rotating your wrist down, and you close the throttle to slow down by rotating your wrist up.

Valve—A mushroom-shaped piece of metal that lets in or keeps out air or fuel, or both. The valve inside a carburetor lets in fuel and air to the engine from the fuel tank and air box. There are two kinds of valves inside an engine. **Intake** valves allow air and fuel into the combustion chamber. **Exhaust** valves let the burned gases out of the combustion chamber.

Valve Gear—The type of system that the engine uses to operate its valves.

Water Cooling System—A water cooling system uses a water/antifreeze mixture that flows through a radiator, cooling off the water. The water then flows through the engine, keeping temperatures inside from getting too hot.

INDEX